Redeemed

SONGS FOR THE SOUL-WINNING CHURCH

ARRANGED BY
MIKE SPECK AND CLIFF DUREN

CREATED BY
MIKE SPECK

ORCHESTRATED BY
DANNY ZALOUDIK, CHRIS MCDONALD, RUSSELL MAULDIN, AND WAYNE HAUN

MIKE SPECK
MUSIC

lillenas
PUBLISHING COMPANY

lillenas.com

CONTENTS

Giving Thanks

with
Thank You, Lord
Give Thanks

Words and Music by
EULALIA KING and
JEFFERY S. FERGUSON
*Arr. by Mike Speck
and Cliff Duren*

PLEASE NOTE: Copying of this product is NOT covered by CCLI licenses. For CCLI information call 1-800-234-2446.

15 thanks. I come re - joic - ing as I

17 en - ter His gates.___ My soul will tes - ti - fy___ that

19 God is so great.___ I can't con - tain this

*"Thank You, Lord"

*Words and Music by ANDRAE CROUCH. © 1971 by BudJohn Songs, Inc./BMI. Administered by EMI CMG. All rights reserved. Used by permission.

46

thanks._____

Thank You for the mer - cy that You show_

B♭   F♯   B   N.C.

48

____ me ev - 'ry-day.____

Thank You for the an - gels that pro-tect_

C♯7   F♯

50

____ me on__ my way.

Thank You for the blood_ that has washed_

F♯m/D♯   E

Let Us Sing

with
He Lives
O for a Thousand Tongues to Sing
O Worship the King

Words and Music by
DWIGHT BROCK
and **J. R. BAXTER**
*Arr. by Mike Speck
and Cliff Duren*

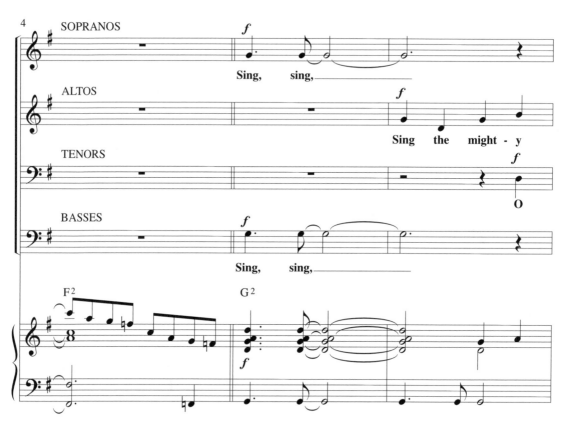

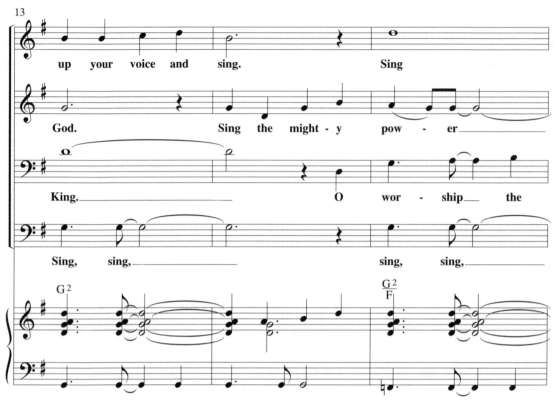

25 *"He Lives"

joice, re - joice O Chris - tian!___ lift up your voice and sing_____ E - ter - nal hal - le - lu - jahs___ to Je - sus Christ, the

CD: 10

22

*"O for a Thousand Tongues to Sing"

for a thou-sand tongues to sing our great Re-deem-er's praise. The

glo - ries of my God and King. O

**"O Worship the King"

wor - ship__ the King, All glo - rious__ a -

Blood-Bought Church

Words and Music by
NANCY HARMON
*Arr. by Mike Speck
and Cliff Duren*

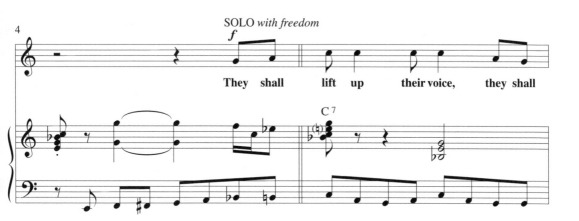

PLEASE NOTE: Copying of this product is NOT covered by CCLI licenses. For CCLI information call 1-800-234-2446.

CD: 17

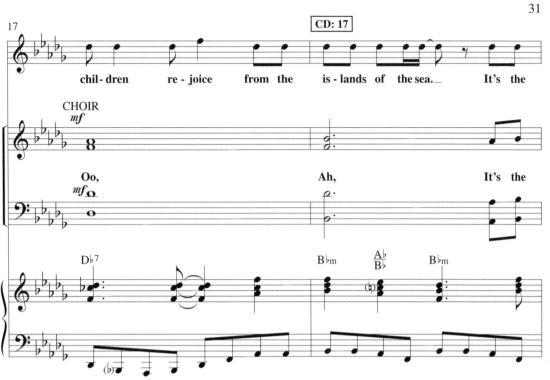

chil - dren re - joice from the is - lands of the sea. _ It's the

CHOIR
mf

Oo, Ah, It's the

mf

D♭7 B♭m A♭/B♭ B♭m

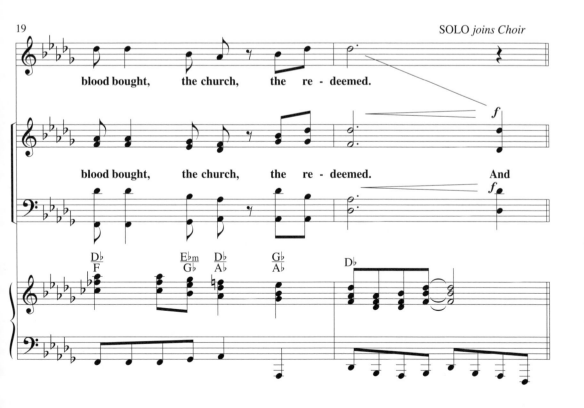

SOLO *joins Choir*

blood bought, the church, the re - deemed.

f

blood bought, the church, the re - deemed. And

f

D♭/F E♭m/G♭ D♭/A♭ G♭/A♭ D♭

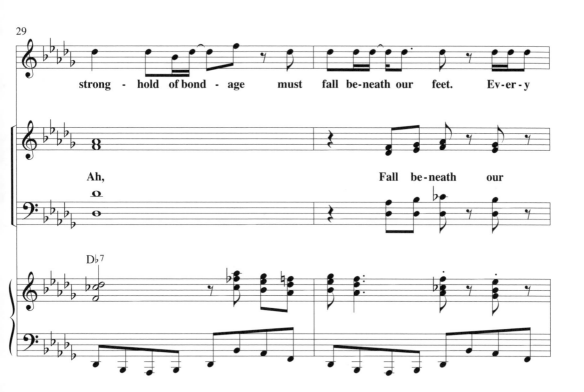

SOLO *continues*

blood bought, the church, the re - deemed.   Let the

blood bought, the church, the re - deemed.

earth keep si - lent, the winds cease to blow,__ Ev-er-y

cre - a - ted be-ing__ fold your wings;   For there's a

new song be-ing sung with a new_____ mel-o-dy,_____ It's the

CHOIR
mf
Oo,
mf
Ah,
It's the

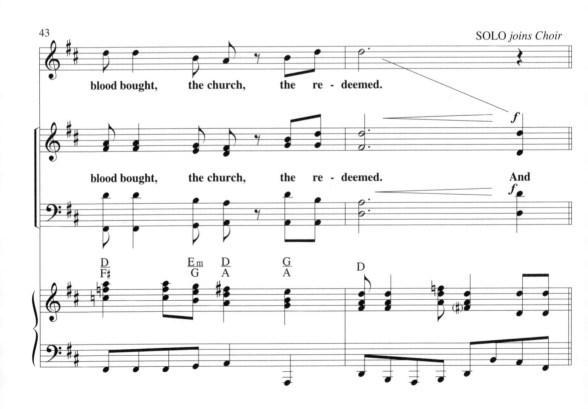

blood bought, the church, the re - deemed.

blood bought, the church, the re - deemed. And

SOLO *joins Choir*

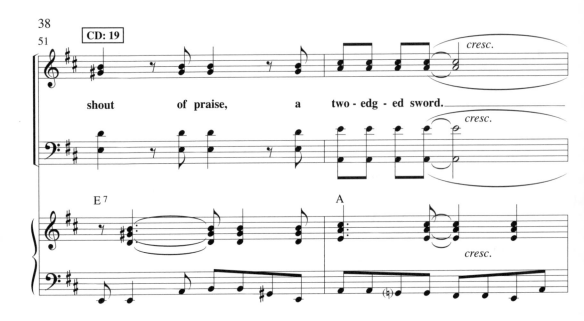

shout of praise, a two-edg-ed sword.

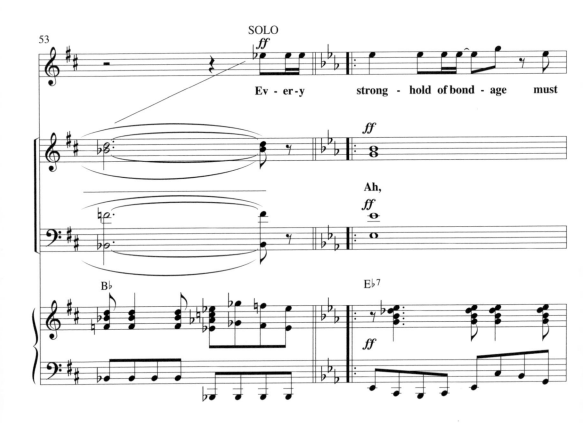

SOLO

Ev-er-y strong-hold of bond-age must

Ah,

fall be-neath our feet. Ev-er-y pris-'ner held cap-tive___ must be___

Fall be-neath our feet.

Eb7

___ free. When our___ de - liv - er-ance___ has come thro' the

Must___ be free, for de - liv - er-ance___ has come thro' the

Bb7

Eb

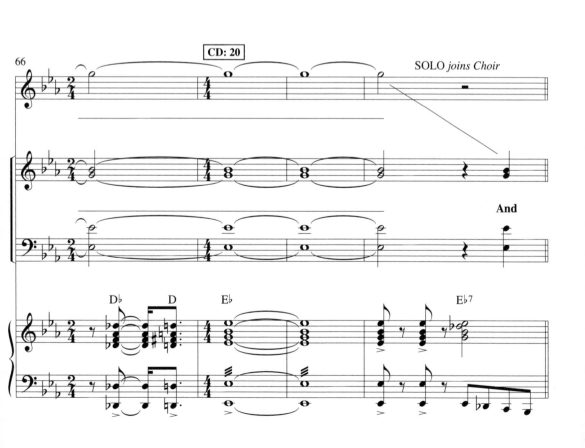

(to pg. 38, meas. 54)

I Am Redeemed

with
Redeemed
Victory in Jesus

Words and Music by
PHIL CROSS
*Arr. by Mike Speck
and Cliff Duren*

PLEASE NOTE: Copying of this product is NOT covered by CCLI licenses. For CCLI information call 1-800-234-2446.

loosed the chains of sin and set me free. I am re-

deemed! I am re-deemed! Je - sus

CD: 23

loosed the chains of sin and set me free.

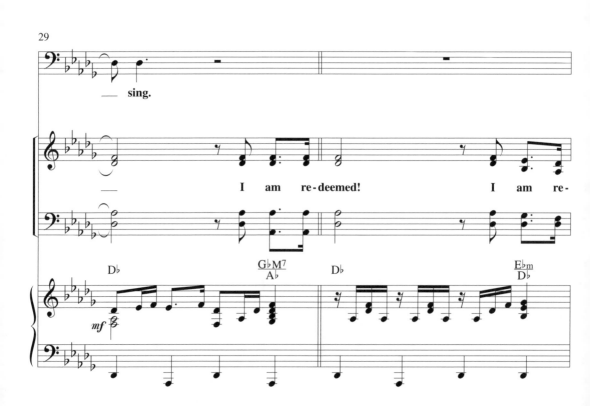

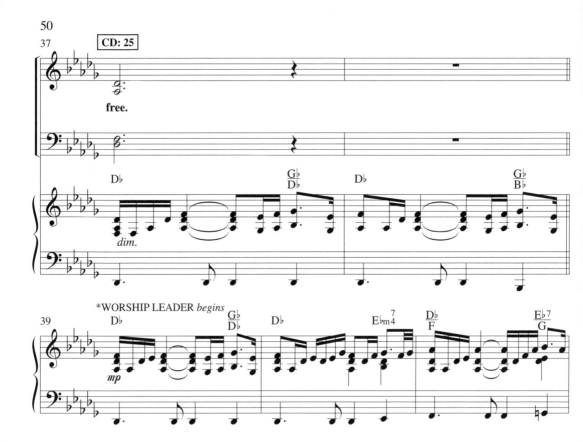

*WORSHIP LEADER: Some glorious morning they will come from all nations, from every generation. Side by side they will march into the celestial city of Jehovah. And in perfect harmony they will begin humming a new song, a song composed by God. Arranged for His children as the "saved by grace" approach the land of their dreams, the host of Heaven will step aside. Even the angels will be silent for they cannot sing this new song. For it is a song reserved for the voices who once cried out for the Redeemer, those washed in the blood of the precious Lamb of God.

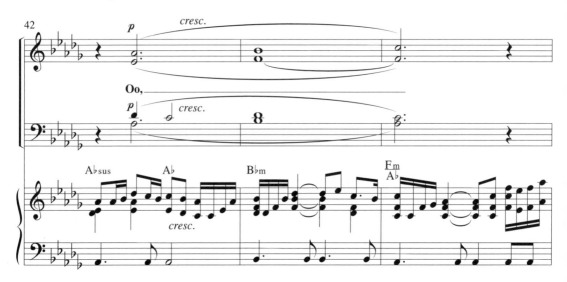

51

CD: 26

Hallelujah for the Cross

with
Glory to His Name
My Savior's Love
Had It Not Been
I Will Glory in the Cross
The Old Rugged Cross Made the Difference

Words and Music by
MARK MATHES
*Arr. by Mike Speck
and Cliff Duren*

14

CD: 30

bore my bur - den to Cal - v'ry, And suf - fered and died a -

Cb   Ebm/C F7#5   Bbm7   Ebm   Cbm6/D   Gb/Db   Db7sus   Db7

*"Hallelujah for the Cross"
A little faster ♩ = ca. 64

17

mf

lone.   O hal - le - lu - jah   for the___

Gb   GbM7   Cb/Gb   Gb   Cb/Gb

cresc.   mf a little faster

19

___cross;   Grace a - vails   for sin - ners___ lost.   For my___

Gb   Gb/F   Cb/Eb   Gb/Db   Ab/C   Cb/Db

*"The Old Rugged Cross Made the Difference"

63

Some Things Never Change

Words and Music by
STEVE HURTE
and GREG DAY
*Arr. by Mike Speck
and Cliff Duren*

I'm not wor-ried in my soul where this old world__ may go, or what I

PLEASE NOTE: Copying of this product is NOT covered by CCLI licenses. For CCLI information call 1-800-234-2446.

an - swer for this mod - ern day._____ Old
saints are still pray - in' and sin-ners who are stray - in' are re-
ceiv - ing God's sav - ing grace._____ Yes, the

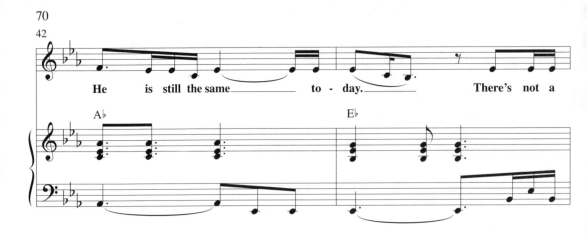

He is still the same_____ to - day._____ There's not a

dif -f'rent ap-proach, it re - mains as He wrote and it

can't be ex - plained_____ a - way._____ They may

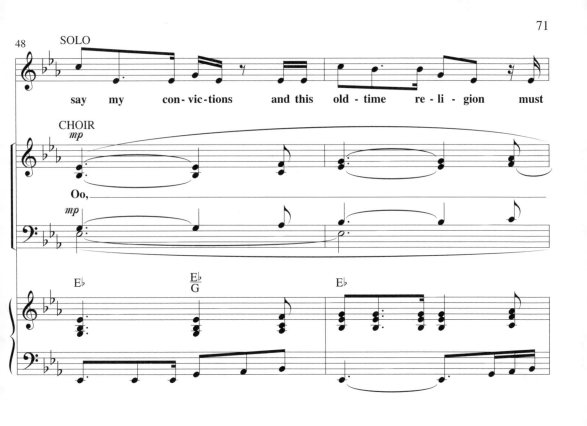

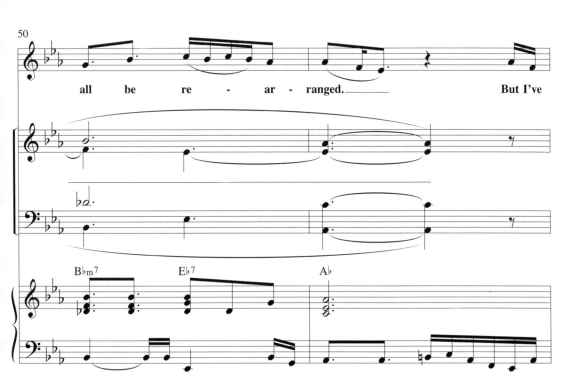

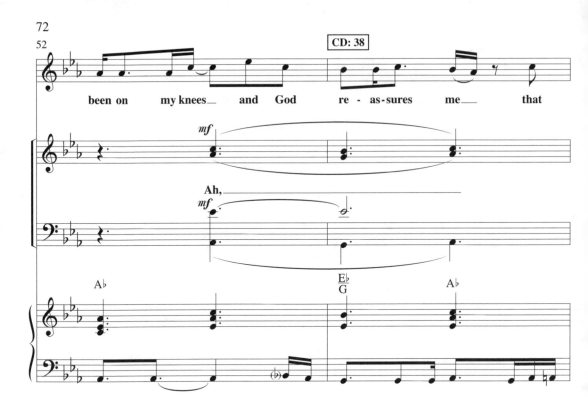

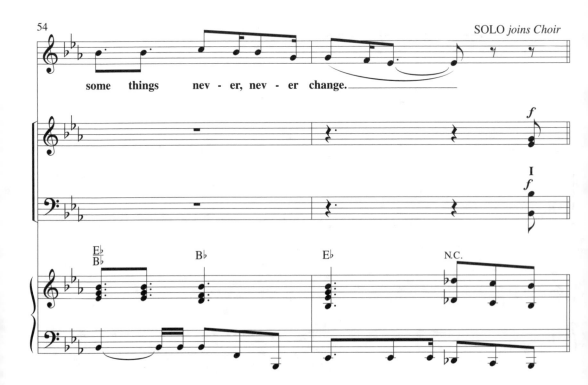

lost, _____ sav - ing the lost. Thank

God some things nev - er change. _____

We Are God's Church

with
I'm in This Church
How Firm a Foundation
The Church Triumphant
The Family of God

Words and Music by
NILES BOROP
and REBECCA PECK
*Arr. by Mike Speck
and Cliff Duren*

CD: 42

*"How Firm a Foundation"

Christ Arose

with

He's Alive
What the Lord Has Done in Me

Words and Music by
ROBERT LOWRY
*Arr. by Mike Speck
and Cliff Duren*

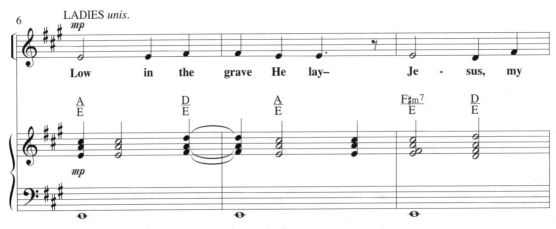

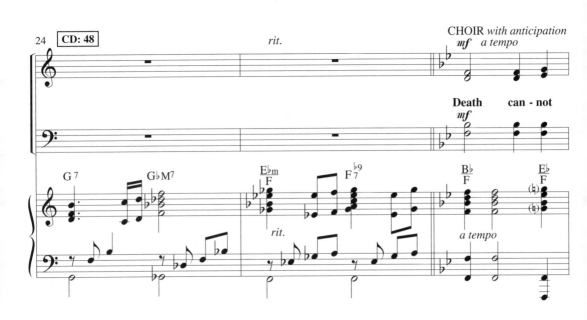

96

He's Not Here

Words and Music by
JAMES MICHAEL SAGE
*Arr. by Mike Speck
and Cliff Duren*

son. He's not here._____ He is ris - en!_____

LADIES *unis.*

mf

Mar - y, re-joic - ing,__ ran back down the hill__ To

D

tell the great - est sto - ry that she would ev - er tell.__ Three

A   G   A

CD: 56

f

days a - go__ at Cal-v'ry cru - ci - fied.__ Now, praise

f

D   B m   G

God for-ev-er-more, He's a-live! He's not

here. He a-rose just like He said. He's not

here. You won't find Him a-mong the dead. He's not

*Second time, don't play on the first (downbeat) eighth note but accent the second eighth note.

Unto the Hills

with

Sheltered in the Arms of God
My Father Watches Over Me
He Hideth My Soul
Under His Wings

Words and Music by
TIM LOVELACE and
JERRY THOMPSON
*Arr. by Mike Speck
and Cliff Duren*

Tenderly ♩ = ca. 78

CD: 59

SOLO 1 *with freedom*

When my plans have fal - len through and I

don't know what to do, I just look un - to the

PLEASE NOTE: Copying of this product is NOT covered by CCLI licenses. For CCLI information call 1-800-234-2446.

20

*"Sheltered in the Arms of God"

*Words and Music by DOTTIE RAMBO and JIMMY DAVIS. © 1969, 1997 Peermusic, Ltd. All rights reserved. Used by permission.

116

NOTE: "Great Is Thy Faithfulness" was featured before the next song in the live concert. We recommend that if desired, it be sung congregationally from a hymnal arrangement with live accompaniment.

You Were There

with
The Unseen Hand

Words and Music by
MARTY FUNDERBURK
and **SCOTT WILEMON**
Arr. by Mike Speck
and Cliff Duren

Wea-ry from the tri-als that it seemed I faced a-lone.

Wan-d'ring why God left me here to strug-gle on my own.

121

"You were there___ for Mos - es, You were there___

CHOIR
mp
"You were there,_____ You were there,___

mel. *mp*

E sus

A

16

for Jo - seph; You were there___ for Da -

You were there___

F♯m

D

-vid when He did - n't have___ a prayer.___ You were there___

when He did - n't have___ a prayer.___ You were there,___

mel.

D

A/E

E sus

19

___ for Steph - en, so I be-lieve_____ in time___ I'll

Oo,_____

A

F♯m

A/E

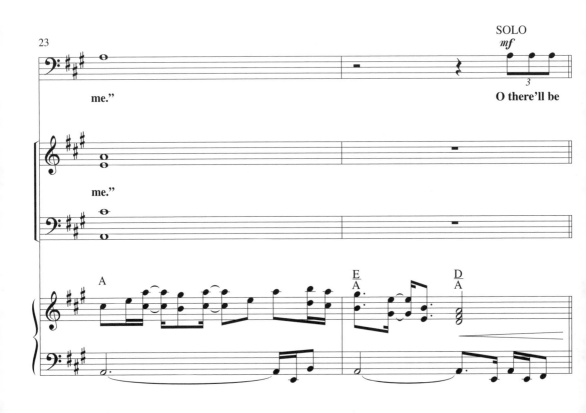

31

saints who've gone be-fore me, may my faith be one more

CD: 68

sto - ry of a life that's lived for Your glo - ry so that

34

oth - ers will be-lieve. You were there for Mos-

CHOIR
mf

You were there,

mel. *mf*

es, You were there_____ for Jo - seph; You were there__

You were there,_____ You were there__

A   F#m

for Da - vid   when He did - n't have__ a prayer.__

when He did - n't have__ a prayer.

mel.

D   A/E

You were there_____ for Steph - en, so I be-lieve__

You were there,_____ Oo,_____

in time__ I'll_____ see That thro' it all,__

CD: 69

cresc.

cresc.

Thro' it all,__

cresc.

cresc.

I will trust in You and hold on to that same un - seen

Ah,

A   Bm7   A/C#   G

47

hand!   I'm trust-ing

the   un - seen   hand!   I'm trust-ing

E sus   F sus   F   Eb/F

49

to

O_____ the un - seen hand_____

a tempo

to

the un - seen hand

that guides me

Bb   D7sus   D7/F#   Gm   F   Eb

51   **CD: 70**

that guides_____ me thro' this wea - ry land.

through.

Bb/D   Gm7   F

You were there_____ for Mos - es, You were there

You were there_____ for Mos - es, You were there

mel. You were there_____ for Mos - es, You were there

G^7_{sus} C

54

_____ for Jo - seph; You were there_____ for Da -

_____ for Jo - seph; You were there_____ for Da -

_____ for Jo - seph; You were there_____ for Da -

A m7 FM9

The Race

Words and Music by
LOIS JANE WALLACE
*Arr. by Mike Speck
and Cliff Duren*

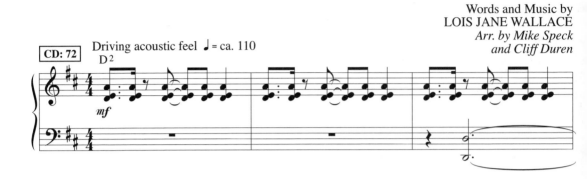

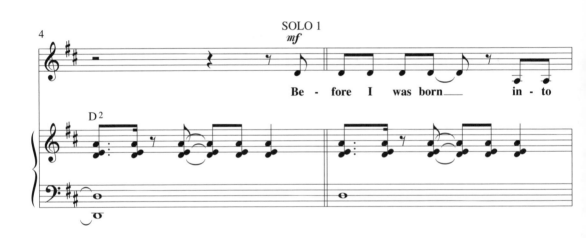

17

knew all a - bout___ me, You tho't I had worth. I was

G² D² A D²

19

CD: 74

called out to serve___ You, do Your king - dom work.___ And

D² A D²

21

SOLO *joins Altos (melody)*

all of my days___ are writ - ten down in Your book.___

CHOIR *f*

mel.

I'm

f

G² D² A D²

run - nin' the race___ and I'm gon - na fin -

ish.___

CD: 75

SOLO 3

Well, I've fal - len down___ in

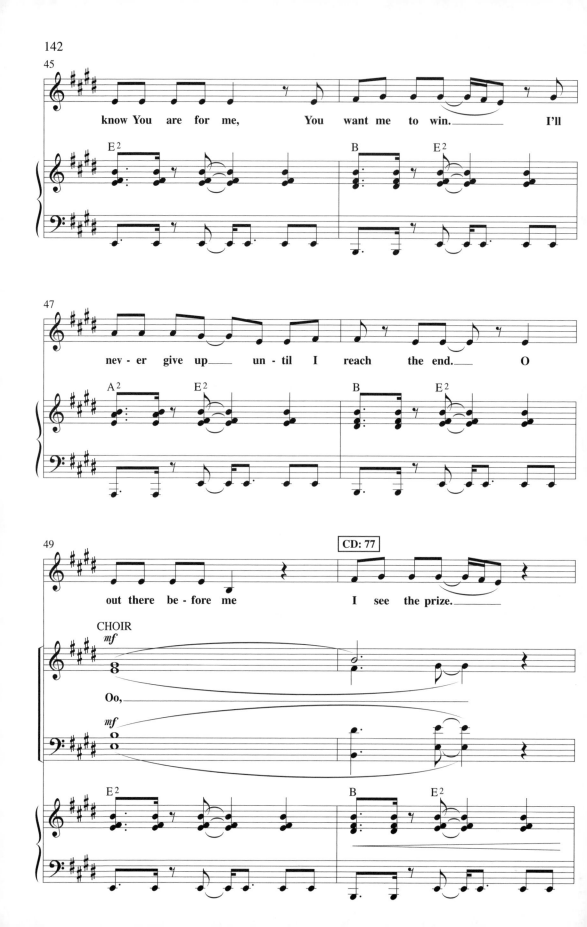

TRIO *joins Choir (SAT)*

Lyrics:
I'm gon - na fin - ish. I'm run - nin' the race ___ and

I, I'm gon - na fin - ish. ___

There Is a Remedy

with

There Is a Balm in Gilead

Words and Music by
ANNIE McRAE
*Arr. by Mike Speck
and Cliff Duren*

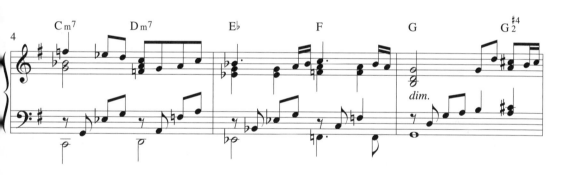

Lyrics:
pain and hurt__ and wrong. There is a so - lu - tion__ for all the
prob-lems deep__ in - side. There is a rem-e-dy and His name is Je - sus
Christ.

CD: 82

SOLO
mf

For the lit - tle, for the lone - ly, for the

G   G²

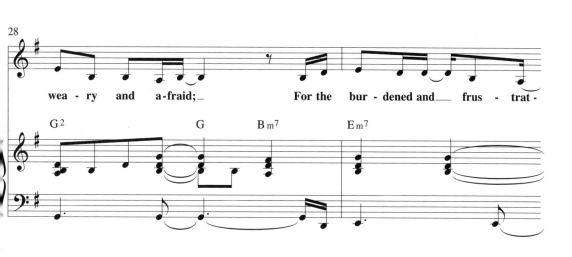

wea - ry and a - fraid;__ For the bur - dened and__ frus - trat -

G²   G   B m7   E m7

- ed, the dis - cour - aged and__ dis - mayed;_____ For the

E m7   A m4⁷   D⁹sus

31

CD: 83

mocked and per-se-cut-ed, for the bat-tered, for the wronged;

G²

For the scarred and for the wound-ed, for the

G² C²/E

34

SOLO *joins Choir*

weak and for the strong

CHOIR *f*

There is a rem-e-dy for

f

D⁷sus G

f

36
ev - 'ry sin - sick soul. There is a cure for all, for all the
G
Em7
38
pain and hurt and wrong. There is a so - lu - tion for all the
Em7
C6 9
40
CD: 84
prob-lems deep in - side. There is a rem - e - dy and His name is Je - sus
C6 9
E♭
F

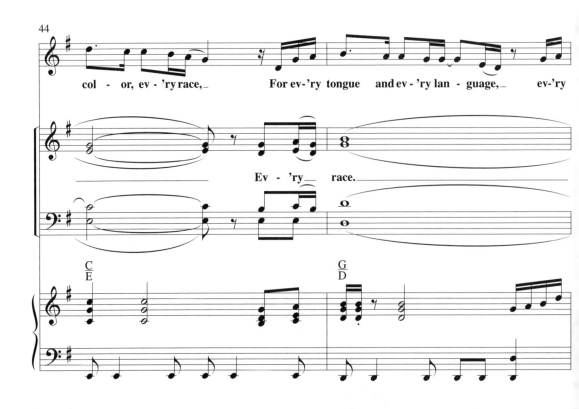

time and ev - 'ry place___ There's an an - swer to___the ques - tion. There's a

Ah,___

love for all the hate.__ There's a heal - er for___ the dy - ing.__ He's the

There's a heal - er for___ the dy - ing.__ He's the

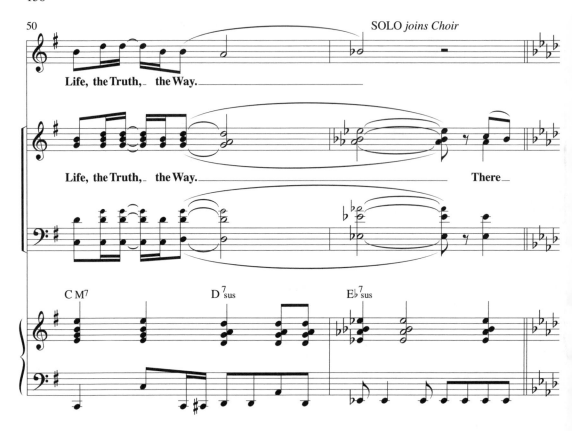

cure for all,___ for all the pain and hurt___ and wrong. There is a so-

lu - tion___ for all the prob-lems deep___ in - side. There is a

rem-e-dy and His name is Je - sus Christ. There is a

Blood-Bought Church (Reprise)

Words and Music by
NANCY HARMON
*Arr. by Mike Speck
and Cliff Duren*

washed in the blood__ and we are go-ing forth. There is

washed in the blood__ and we are go-ing forth. There is

E♭7

noth-ing that can stop this might-y mov-ing force With a

noth-ing that can stop this might-y mov-ing force With a

A♭　　E♭6/G　　Fm7

shout of praise, a two-edg-ed sword.___ Ev-er-y

shout of praise, a two-edg-ed sword.___

strong-hold of bond-age must fall be-neath_ our feet. Ev-er-y

Ah,

Fall be-neath our

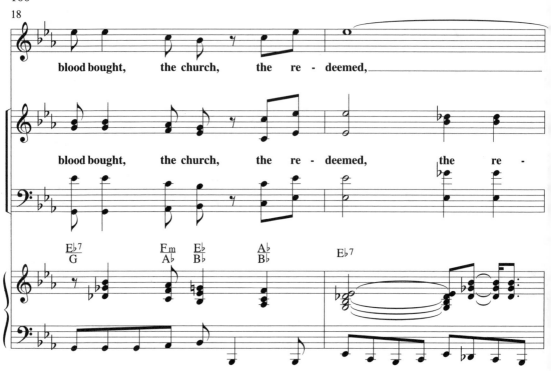

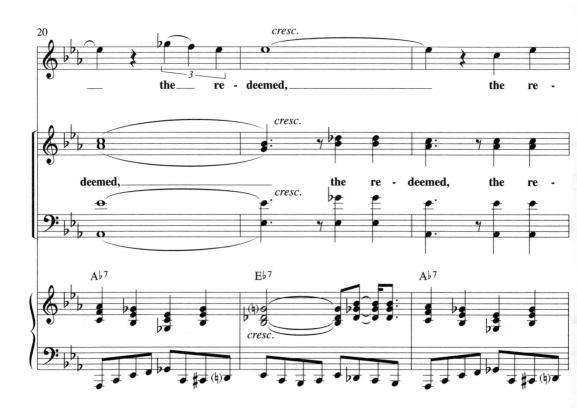

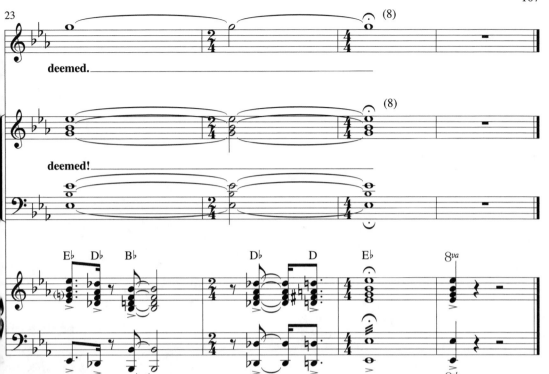

FOR INFORMATION AND BOOKINGS CONTACT:

Mike Speck Ministries

P. O. Box 2609

Lebanon, TN 37088

(615) 449-1888